# DEFINING MOMENTS IN CANADIAN HISTORY

## THE JAPANESE
# INTERNMENT

Weigl

Published by Weigl Educational Publishers Limited
6325 10th Street SE
Calgary, Alberta  T2H 2Z9
Website: www.weigl.ca

All of the Internet URLs given in the book were valid at the time of publication.
However, due to the dynamic nature of the Internet, some addresses may have changed,
or sites may have ceased to exist since publication. While the author and publisher
regret any inconvenience this may cause readers, no responsibility for any such
changes can be accepted by either the author or the publisher.

Library and Archives Canada Cataloguing-in-Publication Data available upon request.
Fax (403) 233-7769 for the attention of the Publishing Records department.

ISBN 978-1-77071-688-9

Printed in the United States of America in North Mankato, Minnesota
1 2 3 4 5 6 7 8 9 0  15 14 13 12 11

072011
WEP040711

Senior Editor: Heather Kissock
Art Director: Terry Paulhus

Every reasonable effort has been made to trace ownership and to obtain permission to
reprint copyright material.

The publishers would be pleased to have any errors or omissions brought to their
attention so that they may be corrected in subsequent printings.

We acknowledge the financial support of the Government of Canada through the
Canada Book Fund for our publishing activities.

# Contents

# Overview

On December 7, 1941, military forces of the Empire of Japan launched a surprise attack on the United States naval base at Pearl Harbor in Hawaii. On the world's stage, this drove the United States into World War II. In Canada, which was already at war, the government used the power authorized by the 1914 **War Measures Act** to remove the entire Japanese Canadian community from British Columbia. Nearly 22,000 Canadians, three-fourths of them either native born or **naturalized citizens**, were forced from their homes and required to live under harsh conditions as prisoners of the government. Their property was sold, usually at a loss, and used by the government to fund their imprisonment. It was 1949 before Japanese Canadians could again move freely throughout Canada.

# Background Information

**Keiko Mary Kitagawa** – A second-generation Japanese Canadian, Mary and her family were uprooted from their home on Salt Spring Island, near Vancouver Island, and spent the 1940s in a number of different **internment** camps and on the sugar beet farms of southern Alberta.

**Tatsuro "Buck" Suzuki** – A commercial salmon fisherman who served with the Canadian army in Asia during World War II, Buck became an early activist for salmon conservation.

**Prime Minister W. L. Mackenzie King** – Canada's prime minister during World War II, he was ultimately responsible for the decision to imprison the Japanese Canadians as "**enemy aliens**" during World War II.

**Prime Minister Brian Mulroney** – While serving as the Prime Minister of Canada, he issued the formal apology to Japanese Canadians on September 22, 1988.

RESENTMENT OF JAPANESE CANADIANS DID NOT BEGIN WITH THE BOMBING OF PEARL HARBOR. IT HAD BEEN THERE SINCE JAPANESE FIRST **IMMIGRATED** TO CANADA.

MAMA, WHY ARE WE BEING TREATED LIKE THIS? WHAT HAVE WE DONE?

WE HAVE DONE NOTHING, NANAKO. THIS IS ABOUT RACISM, ABOUT BEING DIFFERENT. WE ARE FROM JAPAN, NOT EUROPE. WE LOOK DIFFERENT FROM OTHER CANADIANS. OUR CULTURE IS DIFFERENT, OUR LANGUAGE IS DIFFERENT, AND OUR RELIGION IS DIFFERENT.

THE FIRST JAPANESE IMMIGRANTS ARRIVED IN CANADA IN THE LATE 1870S. THEY SETTLED IN VANCOUVER, VICTORIA, AND OTHER COMMUNITIES ALONG CANADA'S WESTERN COAST.

THEY BOUGHT BOATS AND BECAME FISHERMEN. THEY WORKED IN SAW AND PULP MILLS, IN CANNERIES, AND IN MINING. SOME ESTABLISHED FARMS IN THE FRASER VALLEY.

THIS IS HARD WORK, BUT IT WILL ALLOW US TO MAKE A GOOD LIFE FOR OUR CHILDREN.

THE FIRST IMMIGRANTS, WHO HAD BEEN BORN IN JAPAN, WERE CALLED *ISSEI*. THOSE WHO WERE BORN IN CANADA BUT RAISED BY ISSEI PARENTS WERE SECOND GENERATION CANADIANS, CALLED *NISEI*.

I WAS BORN IN JAPAN BUT MY CHILD IS *NISEI*. HE WAS BORN HERE IN THIS COUNTRY. CANADA IS HIS HOME, AND HE WILL ALWAYS BE A CANADIAN CITIZEN.

WE OFTEN EXPERIENCED RESENTMENT, OR RACISM, OVER THE YEARS.

WOULD YOU TELL ME ABOUT IT? IT WOULD MAKE DOING LAUNDRY MORE PLEASANT.

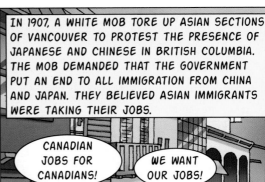

IN 1907, A WHITE MOB TORE UP ASIAN SECTIONS OF VANCOUVER TO PROTEST THE PRESENCE OF JAPANESE AND CHINESE IN BRITISH COLUMBIA. THE MOB DEMANDED THAT THE GOVERNMENT PUT AN END TO ALL IMMIGRATION FROM CHINA AND JAPAN. THEY BELIEVED ASIAN IMMIGRANTS WERE TAKING THEIR JOBS.

CANADIAN JOBS FOR CANADIANS!

WE WANT OUR JOBS!

SEND 'EM BACK WHERE THEY CAME FROM!

NOW HIRING NO JAPANESE

BRITISH COLUMBIA PLACED RESTRICTIONS ON THE LIVES OF JAPANESE CANADIANS. WE WERE NOT ALLOWED IN MANY PROFESSIONS. JAPANESE PEOPLE COULD NOT BECOME CIVIL SERVANTS OR TEACHERS AND WERE OFTEN PAID MUCH LESS THAN OTHER CANADIANS WHO DID THE SAME WORK. JAPANESE CANADIANS WERE NOT ALLOWED TO VOTE.

AS A RESULT, WE CREATED OUR OWN COMMUNITIES HERE IN BRITISH COLUMBIA. WE BUILT OUR OWN STORES, SCHOOLS, HOSPITALS, TEMPLES, AND CHURCHES. WE *NISEI*, BORN AND EDUCATED IN CANADA, WERE FLUENT IN ENGLISH. WE THOUGHT OF OURSELVES AS CANADIANS. IN 1936, WE ASKED FOR THE RIGHT TO VOTE. IT WAS DENIED US.

BEGINNING IN 1931, THE JAPANESE EMPIRE MOVED INTO PARTS OF CHINA. NEWS OF JAPANESE **MILITARISM** IN CHINA INCREASED FEAR AND RESENTMENT IN BRITISH COLUMBIA OF JAPANESE CANADIANS WHO LIVED THERE.

JAPANESE CANADIANS CONTINUED TO LIVE QUIETLY, BUT HOSTILITY TOWARD THEM GREW.

LOOK, IT'S MORE OF THEM JAPS. I'LL BET THEY'RE SPIES FOR THE EMPEROR OF JAPAN.

DO NOT **PROVOKE** THEM. LET'S JUST GET OUT OF HERE QUIETLY.

IN 1939, THE WAR MEASURES ACT WAS REACTIVATED BY THE GOVERNMENT.

THE WAR MEASURES ACT, PASSED IN 1914, WAS IMPORTANT IN DEFENDING OUR NATION DURING WORLD WAR I. WE WILL NEED IT AGAIN.

THE WAR MEASURES ACT LET THE GOVERNMENT, IN A CRISIS SITUATION, TAKE AWAY THE RIGHTS AND FREEDOMS OF ANY GROUP SUSPECTED OF BEING A DANGER TO THE NATIONAL SECURITY OF CANADA. DURING WORLD WAR I, THE GOVERNMENT USED IT AGAINST UKRAINIAN CANADIANS. NOW, THE GOVERNMENT WAS PREPARING TO USE IT AGAINST JAPANESE CANADIANS.

WELL, THEY DID IT. THEY BROUGHT BACK THE WAR MEASURES ACT.

IT'S ONLY A MATTER OF TIME UNTIL IT IS USED AGAINST US. WHAT HAVE WE DONE TO BRING THIS ABOUT?

11

ON DECEMBER 7, 1941, JAPAN LAUNCHED A SUDDEN, DEVASTATING ATTACK ON THE UNITED STATES NAVY BASED AT PEARL HARBOR IN HAWAII.

ALMOST IMMEDIATELY, THE PAPERS AND RADIO WERE FILLED WITH DREADFUL NEWS. PACIFIC POSSESSIONS OF THE UNITED STATES AND GREAT BRITAIN WERE ATTACKED AND FELL TO JAPANESE FORCES.

THE WAR IN THE PACIFIC CONTINUES TO GO BADLY. THE H.M.S. *PRINCE OF WALES* AND H.M.S. *REPULSE* WERE SUNK YESTERDAY, DECEMBER 10.

WHAT IS HAPPENING IN THE WORLD?

WHAT WILL HAPPEN TO US?

TODAY AT SCHOOL, A BOY CALLED ME A JAP AND SAID WE ARE ALL SPIES FOR JAPAN. THAT'S SILLY—I'M CANADIAN, NOT JAPANESE.

HATRED IS BOILING OVER. WHAT WILL BECOME OF US?

NEWS

Hong Kong Falls on Christmas Day, 1941

2000 Canadian soldiers killed or captured

THE REACTION IN CANADA WAS SWIFT AND HARSH. THE DAY AFTER THE BOMBING OF PEARL HARBOR, THE ROYAL CANADIAN NAVY IN BRITISH COLUMBIA **IMPOUNDED** MORE THAN 1,200 JAPANESE FISHING VESSELS.

BUT WE FISH FOR A LIVING. HOW CAN WE WORK WITHOUT OUR BOAT? HOW CAN WE FEED OUR FAMILIES?

THAT'S NOT MY PROBLEM. I'M JUST DOING MY JOB.

IN A MEETING THE DAY AFTER PEARL HARBOR, PRIME MINISTER KING EXPRESSED CONCERN FOR THE SAFETY OF JAPANESE CANADIANS.

THE ANTI-JAPANESE DEMONSTRATIONS IN BRITISH COLUMBIA MAY PLACE OUR JAPANESE CANADIAN CITIZENS IN DANGER, BUT I HAVE EVERY CONFIDENCE IN THEIR LOYALTY.

RACISM AND HOSTILITY GREW AGAINST JAPANESE CANADIANS. THERE WERE SUGGESTIONS THAT THEY WERE A NATIONAL SECURITY RISK.

YOU KNOW THE GOVERNMENT TOOK ALL THEIR BOATS AWAY AS A DEFENSIVE MEASURE.

THE GOVERNMENT WOULDN'T HAVE DONE THAT IF THE JAPANESE WEREN'T A SECURITY RISK. THEY PROBABLY ALL WORKED FOR THE JAPANESE NAVY.

BY DECEMBER 16, A LAW WAS PASSED REQUIRING ALL PERSONS OF JAPANESE ANCESTRY, WHATEVER THEIR NATIONALITY, TO REGISTER WITH THE GOVERNMENT AS ENEMY ALIENS. THAT MEANT CHILDREN, ADULTS, AND THE ELDERLY.

I'M TOO OLD FOR THIS. BESIDES, I AM A NATURALIZED CANADIAN CITIZEN.

I DON'T UNDERSTAND WHY I HAVE TO DO THIS. I WAS BORN HERE. I AM A CANADIAN CITIZEN.

ON JANUARY 16, 1942, USING THE AUTHORITY OF THE WAR MEASURES ACT, A 100-MILE LINE WAS DRAWN. THIS MADE A "PROTECTED AREA" EXTENDING 160 KM EASTWARD FROM THE PACIFIC COAST OF BRITISH COLUMBIA.

WHY WOULD ANYONE THINK WE ARE THE ENEMY?

IN EARLY FEBRUARY, THE GOVERNMENT BEGAN TO REMOVE "ENEMY ALIENS" FROM THIS "PROTECTED AREA." THEY STARTED WITH MEN BETWEEN THE AGES OF 18 AND 45.

IN LATE FEBRUARY, THE MINISTER OF JUSTICE WAS GIVEN AUTHORITY TO CONTROL THE ACTIVITIES OF ALL JAPANESE CANADIANS IN THE "PROTECTED AREA." THEN THE BRITISH COLUMBIA SECURITY COMMISSION WAS ESTABLISHED. ITS JOB WAS TO SUPERVISE AND DIRECT THE REMOVAL OF JAPANESE CANADIANS FROM BRITISH COLUMBIA.

THE CUSTODIAN OF ENEMY ALIEN PROPERTY WILL TAKE RESPONSIBILITY OF EVERYTHING FOR US.

THE GOVERNMENT HAS TAKEN AWAY ALL OUR CARS, CAMERAS, AND RADIOS.

WE MUST LEAVE HERE TOMORROW. WE ARE ONLY ALLOWED TO TAKE WHAT WE CAN CARRY. WHAT WILL HAPPEN TO EVERYTHING ELSE?

WHERE ARE WE GOING? WHAT SHOULD WE TAKE WITH US?

AS IF THIS DUSK-TO-DAWN *CURFEW* WAS NOT DIFFICULT ENOUGH! HOW CAN WE FIND OUT WHAT'S HAPPENING OUT THERE?

MORE THAN 60 PERCENT OF THESE PEOPLE WERE CANADIAN BORN. ANOTHER 15 PERCENT WERE NATURALIZED CANADIAN CITIZENS. THAT MEANS THAT THREE-FOURTHS OF THESE "ENEMY ALIENS" WERE CANADIAN CITIZENS.

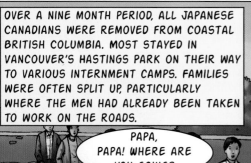

OVER A NINE MONTH PERIOD, ALL JAPANESE CANADIANS WERE REMOVED FROM COASTAL BRITISH COLUMBIA. MOST STAYED IN VANCOUVER'S HASTINGS PARK ON THEIR WAY TO VARIOUS INTERNMENT CAMPS. FAMILIES WERE OFTEN SPLIT UP, PARTICULARLY WHERE THE MEN HAD ALREADY BEEN TAKEN TO WORK ON THE ROADS.

PAPA, PAPA! WHERE ARE YOU GOING?

OH, MY DEAR...WRITE IF YOU CAN.

BE GOOD FOR YOUR MAMA. I LOVE YOU.

MEN SENT TO THE ROAD CAMPS LIVED IN COLD, CROWDED, AND UNCOMFORTABLE CONDITIONS.

I WISH THIS FOOD WOULD STAY WARM LONG ENOUGH TO WARM ME!

AND SO, DEAR FAMILY, I WRITE TO YOU FROM A ROAD CAMP NEAR YELLOWHEAD PASS. IT IS VERY COLD...

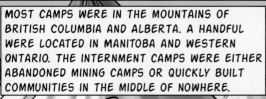

MOST CAMPS WERE IN THE MOUNTAINS OF BRITISH COLUMBIA AND ALBERTA. A HANDFUL WERE LOCATED IN MANITOBA AND WESTERN ONTARIO. THE INTERNMENT CAMPS WERE EITHER ABANDONED MINING CAMPS OR QUICKLY BUILT COMMUNITIES IN THE MIDDLE OF NOWHERE.

MAMA, HOW LONG DO WE HAVE TO LIVE IN THIS TENT?

JUST UNTIL THE CABINS ARE BUILT. I HOPE WE WILL BE IN A CABIN BY WINTER.

AT LEAST WE'RE OUT OF THE ANIMAL STALLS AT HASTINGS PARK.

THE CABINS WERE SMALL AND COLD.

MAMA, I'M SO COLD.

MY BLANKET FROZE TO THE WALL AGAIN LAST NIGHT.

MRS. OSAKA SAID THEY SLEEP WITH LANTERNS UNDER THEIR BEDS TO KEEP WARM.

I HEARD THAT SOME CATHOLIC NUNS ARE GOING TO START A SCHOOL FOR THE CHILDREN HERE.

17

PRIME MINISTER MACKENZIE KING ALSO APPROVED OF A PLAN FOR "VOLUNTARY **REPATRIATION**" OF JAPANESE CANADIANS TO JAPAN.

THIS IS A GOOD PLAN. IT SHOULD MAKE THE VOTERS HAPPY.

THE GOVERNMENT PUSHED THE JAPANESE CANADIANS TO EITHER SIGN PAPERS ALLOWING THEM TO BE SENT TO JAPAN, A COUNTRY MOST OF THEM HAD NEVER SEEN, OR TO MOVE EAST OF THE ROCKIES.

IF YOU WANT TO LEAVE THIS CAMP, YOU NEED TO SIGN THESE PAPERS.

SOME CHOICE. EITHER WAY, WE CAN'T GO BACK HOME.

I DON'T KNOW IF I WANT TO STAY IN A COUNTRY THAT TREATS ME THE WAY I'VE BEEN TREATED THESE PAST FEW YEARS.

IN 1946, CANADA BEGAN DEPORTING EXILED JAPANESE CANADIANS TO JAPAN, A NATION TORN BY THE WAR. ALTHOUGH THE **DEPORTATION** ORDERS WERE CHALLENGED, THE SUPREME COURT UPHELD THEM.

IT WAS 1947 BEFORE THE ORDERS WERE CANCELED. BY THAT TIME 4,000 JAPANESE CANADIANS HAD BEEN SENT TO JAPAN.

IT WAS NOT UNTIL APRIL 1, 1949, THAT ALL RESTRICTIONS AGAINST JAPANESE CANADIANS ENDED. FINALLY, THEY WERE FREE TO MOVE ABOUT CANADA, EVEN TO SETTLE IN BRITISH COLUMBIA.

I DON'T KNOW WHERE WE'LL END UP. WE'VE LOST THE WORK OF A LIFETIME.

WE DON'T HAVE A LIFETIME AHEAD OF US TO REPLACE IT ALL.

WE'RE GOING TO ONTARIO. I'LL NEVER GO BACK TO BRITISH COLUMBIA.

I'M GOING TO BECOME AS CANADIAN AS POSSIBLE. NO MORE JAPANESE CULTURE FOR ME.

THE JAPANESE COMMUNITIES WERE BROKEN UP, AND JAPANESE CANADIANS INTERMARRIED WITH OTHER CANADIANS. MUCH OF THE CULTURAL HERITAGE OF JAPANESE CANADIANS WAS LOST.

## The Story of Mary Kitagawa

MARY GREW UP ON SALT SPRING ISLAND WHERE HER PARENTS HAD WORKED MANY YEARS TO MAKE THEIR SMALL FARM SUCCESSFUL.

MARY'S FATHER, WHO HAD BEEN BORN IN JAPAN, WAS AMONG THE FIRST GROUP OF MEN TAKEN INTO CUSTODY BY THE GOVERNMENT IN EARLY 1942. IT WAS SEVERAL MONTHS BEFORE THE FAMILY KNEW WHAT HAD HAPPENED TO HIM.

WHAT ABOUT MY FAMILY? WHO WILL TAKE CARE OF THEM?

ABOUT A MONTH AFTER HER FATHER WAS TAKEN AWAY, MARY AND HER SIBLINGS, ALONG WITH THEIR MOTHER, WERE ORDERED TO LEAVE.

ARE WE GOING TO BE WITH FATHER?

IF WE MOVE, HOW WILL FATHER FIND US?

DID I BRING EVERYTHING I'LL NEED?

HOW CAN WE POSSIBLY KNOW WHAT WE WILL NEED IF WE DON'T KNOW WHERE WE ARE GOING?

THE KITAGAWAS SPENT A MONTH AT HASTINGS PARK BEFORE BEING TAKEN BY TRAIN TO GREENWOOD, ONE OF THE ABANDONED MINING CAMPS. THERE THEY SLEPT ON THE FLOOR AND COOKED THEIR FOOD IN A COMMUNAL KITCHEN. THEY HAD NO SCHOOL.

I'LL BET THERE ARE MICE.

WHAT A MESS. EITHER THE MINERS LIVED LIKE ANIMALS, OR ANIMALS LIVED HERE AFTER THEM.

I AM VERY TIRED.

20

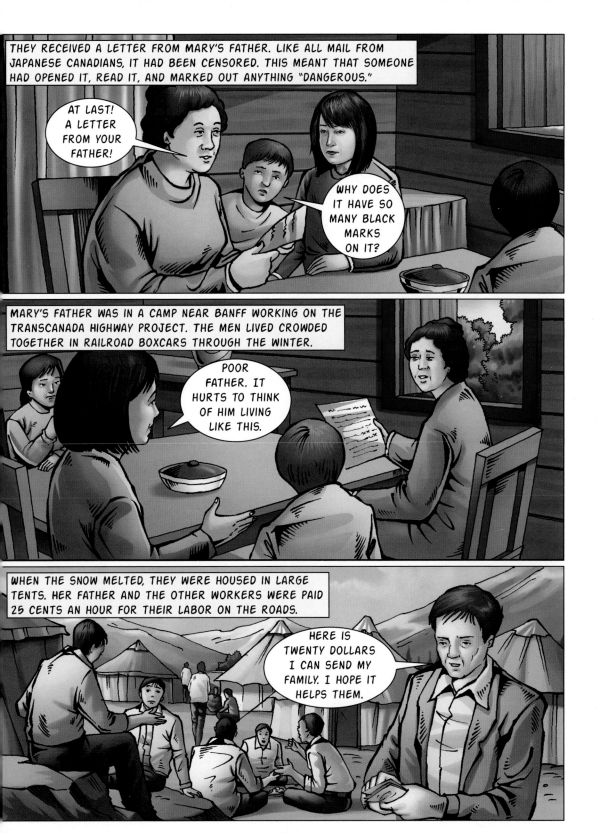

IN ORDER TO BE REUNITED WITH THEIR FATHER, MARY'S FAMILY AGREED TO MOVE TO THE SUGAR BEET FIELDS OF ALBERTA.

IS THAT OUR HOUSE?

I DOUBT IT.

THEIR FIRST "HOME" WAS A 3 METRE BY 4.5 METRE BOX, JUST 3 M FROM THE PIGPEN. MARY'S PARENTS HAD TO BUY A STOVE AND LUMBER TO BUILD A TABLE AND BEDS FOR THE FAMILY. THERE WAS NO KITCHEN AND NO WAY TO STORE FOOD.

WHEN I FINISH THIS, WE CAN HAVE A PLACE TO EAT, AND YOU CHILDREN WILL HAVE SPACE FOR SCHOOL WORK.

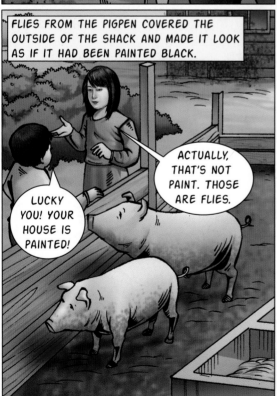

FLIES FROM THE PIGPEN COVERED THE OUTSIDE OF THE SHACK AND MADE IT LOOK AS IF IT HAD BEEN PAINTED BLACK.

ACTUALLY, THAT'S NOT PAINT. THOSE ARE FLIES.

LUCKY YOU! YOUR HOUSE IS PAINTED!

HER FATHER WORKED FOR A FARMER WHO HATED JAPANESE. MARY'S FATHER DROVE A TEAM OF HORSES TO PLOW, CUT, AND HARVEST HAY. MARY'S OLDER SISTER WORKED FOR THE FARMER'S WIFE AND WAS PAID IN MILK AND BUTTER.

THIS WORK IS TOO MUCH FOR HIM. AND OH, HOW I HATE TO HEAR THE FARMER YELL AT HIM DAY AFTER DAY.

AFTER A FEW MONTHS IN THIS SETTING, THE KITAGAWA FAMILY WAS TRANSFERRED TO A CAMP NEAR SLOCAN LAKE. THEY OCCUPIED ONE OF HUNDREDS OF SMALL SHACKS HOUSING EXILED FAMILIES.

EACH SHACK WAS DIVIDED INTO THREE ROOMS, A BEDROOM ON EACH SIDE OF A COMMON ROOM. AS A FAMILY OF SEVEN, THEY HAD AN ENTIRE SHACK TO THEMSELVES. SMALLER FAMILIES HAD TO SHARE SUCH A SPACE.

I'M COLD. THERE IS COLD AIR BLOWING UP ON MY FEET.

IT'S FROM GAPS IN THE FLOORING. THIS SMALL STOVE CAN NEVER KEEP UP WITH THE COLD AIR THAT BLOWS IN.

I DON'T WANT TO THINK ABOUT STILL BEING HERE NEXT WINTER.

MAYBE WE CAN PUT IN SOME INSULATION BEFORE NEXT WINTER.

OVER THE YEARS, THE EXILES PLANTED GARDENS TO GROW FOOD AND IMPROVED THE INSULATION OF THEIR SHACKS. EVENTUALLY, IN MARY'S COMMUNITY, THE SHACKS WERE PROVIDED WITH WATER AND ELECTRICITY.

THIS SHOULD KEEP US WARMER WHEN WINTER COMES.

I USED TO TAKE RUNNING WATER AND ELECTRICITY FOR GRANTED.

SCHOOLS WERE SET UP, AND YOUNG WOMEN SERVED AS TEACHERS FOR THE YOUNGER CHILDREN. THE FATHERS BUILT THE CLASSROOM FURNITURE. MARY'S SISTER HAD TO WALK EIGHT KILOMETERS EACH WAY, TO THE CAMP AT NEW DENVER, TO ATTEND HIGH SCHOOL.

WHEN THE GOVERNMENT SOLD THE KITAGAWA FAMILY FARM, THE MONEY DUE HER PARENTS WAS $500. WHAT THE GOVERNMENT GAVE THE KITAGAWAS FROM THIS EACH MONTH WAS NOT EVEN ENOUGH TO PROVIDE CLOTHING AND SHOES FOR THEIR FAMILY. THEIR FAMILY FARM WAS GONE.

IN 1949, WHEN RESTRICTIONS ON JAPANESE CANADIANS WERE LIFTED, THE FAMILY DECIDED TO GO INTO THE RESTAURANT BUSINESS IN ALBERTA. THEY WORKED HARD FOR FIVE YEARS TO SAVE TOWARD THEIR DREAM OF RETURNING TO SALT SPRING ISLAND.

ON SALT SPRING ISLAND, THE KITAGAWAS TRIED TO BUY THEIR FARM BACK FROM THE VETERAN WHO NOW OWNED IT, BUT HE REFUSED TO SELL.

IT MAY HAVE BEEN YOURS BEFORE THE WAR, BUT IT IS MY FARM NOW.

ALTHOUGH MARY'S PARENTS WERE OVER 50, THEY HAD TO START OVER AGAIN. THEY BOUGHT SOME SCRUBLAND. THE FAMILY WORKED FOR YEARS TO TURN IT INTO A PRODUCTIVE FARM.

**The Story of Tatsuro "Buck" Suzuki**

TATSURO "BUCK" SUZUKI WAS BORN ON DON ISLAND IN THE FRASER RIVER. WHEN THE WAR BEGAN, HE WAS A COMMERCIAL FISHERMAN IN THE FRASER RIVER FISHERY IN BRITISH COLUMBIA.

LIKE OTHER JAPANESE, TATSURO HAD TO LEAVE BRITISH COLUMBIA AFTER THE ATTACK AT PEARL HARBOR. HE MOVED TO ONTARIO. WITH 149 OTHER *NISEI* MEN, TATSURO JOINED THE CANADIAN ARMED FORCES TO SERVE IN THE FAR EAST.

THE BRITISH ARMY HAS ASKED US TO CONTACT YOU AND OTHER *NISEI* TO SERVE IN MILITARY INTELLIGENCE.

I'VE ASKED AND ASKED TO BE ALLOWED TO JOIN THE ARMY.

THE GOVERNMENT ALLOWED THEM TO SERVE IN THE CANADIAN ARMY ONLY BECAUSE THE BRITISH GOVERNMENT WANTED TO ENLIST THEM.

I THOUGHT WE WERE GOING TO BE IN THE BRITISH ARMY.

DIDN'T YOU HEAR? THE GOVERNMENT WOULD NOT HEAR OF US 'ENEMY ALIENS' SERVING UNDER ANYTHING BUT A CANADIAN FLAG.

TATSURO SERVED IN BURMA. HE AND ANOTHER JAPANESE CANADIAN GAVE THE SURRENDER ORDER TO THE JAPANESE FORCES IN SOUTHEAST ASIA.

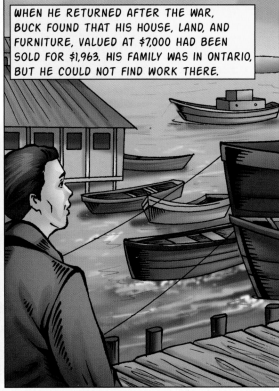

WHEN HE RETURNED AFTER THE WAR, BUCK FOUND THAT HIS HOUSE, LAND, AND FURNITURE, VALUED AT $7,000 HAD BEEN SOLD FOR $1,963. HIS FAMILY WAS IN ONTARIO, BUT HE COULD NOT FIND WORK THERE.

AS A VETERAN, HE WAS FREE TO ENTER BRITISH COLUMBIA, SO HE LAID THE GROUNDWORK FOR JAPANESE FISHERMEN TO RETURN TO FISHING IN APRIL 1949.

THE UNITED FISHERMEN AND ALLIED WORKERS' UNION AGREES TO SUPPORT JAPANESE FISHERMEN WHEN THEY ARE FREE TO RETURN TO BRITISH COLUMBIA.

BUT THEY MUST JOIN OUR UNION RATHER THAN FORMING THEIR OWN.

I AGREE.

SUZUKI BORROWED $2,000 TO BUY AN OLD BOAT AND NET AS WELL AS TO MAKE A DOWN PAYMENT ON LAND AND A HOUSE. HE BECAME AN IMPORTANT ENVIRONMENTALIST IN BRITISH COLUMBIA. HE DIED IN 1977, NEVER HEARING THE GOVERNMENT'S APOLOGY FOR THE WAR YEARS.

WITH A BOAT, I CAN BEGIN TO MAKE SOME MONEY, PAY MY DEBTS, AND MOVE FORWARD.

YOU'LL DO WELL, BUCK!

MY GENERATION LOST OUR HERITAGE BECAUSE OF THE INTERNMENT. MY MOTHER, WHO HAD BEEN A TEENAGER IN THE CAMPS, MOVED TO TORONTO. SHE LEFT BEHIND ALL HER JAPANESE CULTURE AND MARRIED A BRITISH CANADIAN MAN. I KNEW MY MOTHER WAS JAPANESE CANADIAN, BUT SHE NEVER TALKED ABOUT HER PAST.

BEFORE THE WAR, WE *NISEI* HAD NO FUTURE. WE LIVED IN OUR JAPANESE COMMUNITIES IN BRITISH COLUMBIA. WE WERE RESTRICTED TO ONLY A FEW CAREERS. AFTER THE WAR, WE MOVED TO OTHER PARTS OF CANADA. NOW, WE CAN LIVE WHERE WE WANT AND WORK AT WHATEVER CAREER WE WANT. WE, MORE THAN ANY OTHER MINORITY GROUP, HAVE BEEN ABSORBED INTO THE CANADIAN POPULATION.

I DON'T THINK I EVER GOT OVER THE HUMILIATION OF THOSE YEARS. I WAS LABELED AN "ENEMY ALIEN", AND I LOST MY YOUTH. I WAS ROBBED OF MY HERITAGE AND BECAME ASHAMED OF WHO I WAS. THE APOLOGY HELPED, BUT WHY DID ALL THIS HAVE TO HAPPEN TO US?

# Brain Teasers

1. Give three examples of restrictions placed on Japanese Canadians in the years before World War II.

2. What legal authority did the government use to remove Japanese Canadians from British Columbia?

3. What was the War Measures Act?

4. What happened to Japanese Canadian fishermen on December 8, 1941?

5. Give three examples of life in internment camps.

6. What two choices were offered to Japanese Canadians who wanted to leave internment camps at the end of the war?

7. List three ways that the internment changed life for the Japanese Canadian community.

Answers

1. Japanese Canadians were barred from certain jobs, and they were not allowed to vote. Restaurants and public pools were closed to them, and they were not allowed certain theater seats.

2. The government used the War Measures Act of 1914.

3. The act allowed the government to take away the rights and freedoms of any group that was suspected of being a threat to national security if there was a crisis situation. The act was used during both World War I and World War II.

4. Their boats were impounded by the Royal Canadian Navy.

5. People living in internment camps had hard lives. They were forced to live in tents or in cabins that were small, crowded, and dirty. The cabins had no insulation, and it was very cold in the winter. Once schools were organized, young people had to walk a long distance to get to school. Internees had little money, and they had to use what was left of their own money to support themselves.

6. They were offered the choice of being deported to Japan or promising to remain east of the Rockies.

7. The communities were broken up, and Japanese Canadians dispersed into other parts of Canada. Japanese Canadians intermarried with other Canadians and became one of the most completely assimilated minority groups in Canada. Much of the cultural heritage of Japanese Canadians was lost to later generations.

30

# Further Information

**How can I find out more about Japanese internment during World War II?**

Most libraries have computers that connect to a database that contains information on books and articles about different subjects. You can input a key word and find material on the person, place, or thing you want to learn more about. The computer will provide you with a list of books in the library that contain information on the subject you searched for. Non-fiction books are arranged numerically, using their call numbers. Fiction books are organized alphabetically by the author's last name.

## Books

Nakano, Takeo Ujo. *Within the Barbed Wire Fence: A Japanese Man's Account of His Internment in Canada*. University of Toronto Press, 1980. Goodread Biographies, 1983.

Sando, Tom. *Wild Daisies in the Sand: Life in a Canadian Internment Camp*. NeWest Press, 2002.

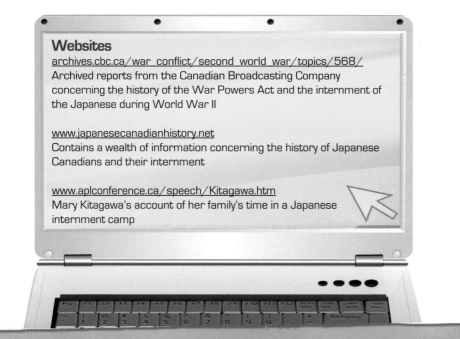

**Websites**

archives.cbc.ca/war_conflict/second_world_war/topics/568/
Archived reports from the Canadian Broadcasting Company concerning the history of the War Powers Act and the internment of the Japanese during World War II

www.japanesecanadianhistory.net
Contains a wealth of information concerning the history of Japanese Canadians and their internment

www.aplconference.ca/speech/Kitagawa.htm
Mary Kitagawa's account of her family's time in a Japanese internment camp

# Glossary

**curfew:** a set hour when businesses must close and people are no longer allowed to be on the streets

**deportation:** removing individuals or certain groups of people from a country

**doles:** hands out in small portions, distributes

**enemy aliens:** citizens of other countries living in Canada who were considered a threat to national security

**immigrated:** settled in a country or region to which one is not native

**impound:** seize and keep in legal custody

**internment:** confinement to a specific location, especially during wartime

**militarism:** government policies that glorify and place great importance on having well prepared military forces

**naturalized citizens:** people who have full citizenship rights in one country, although they were born in another country

**provoke:** make someone angry

**repatriation:** returning to the country where one was born

**resentment:** anger, bad feelings

**sabotage:** deliberate, harmful destruction or damage

**War Measures Act:** passed in 1914, this act allowed the government to assume broad emergency powers in the event or war or invasion

# Index